Being Me

A Keepsake Scrapbook for African American Girls

By Toni Trent Parker

Illustrations by Meryl Treatner

SCHOLASTIC INC.

New York   Toronto   London   Auckland   Sydney
Mexico City   New Delhi   Hong Kong   Buenos Aires

The Basics About Me

The Early Years

I was born in _____on _____ at_____o'clock A.M./P.M.
                      (city and state)   (date)

They tell me I weighed_____pounds_____ounces and was_____inches long.

Everyone says I looked just like_____.

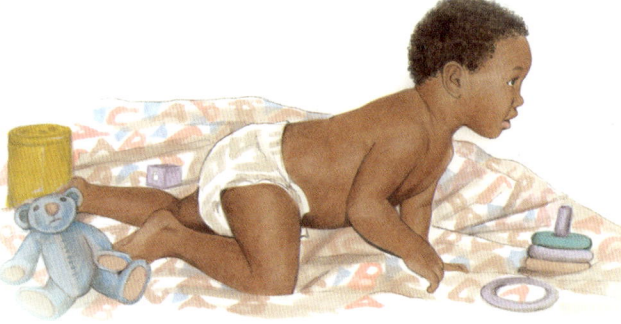

When I was a baby . . .

My name was chosen because_____
_____
_____
_____.

My name means_____
_____
_____
_____
_____
_____
_____
_____
_____.

Place photo here.

Photos of Me

When I was a younger . . .

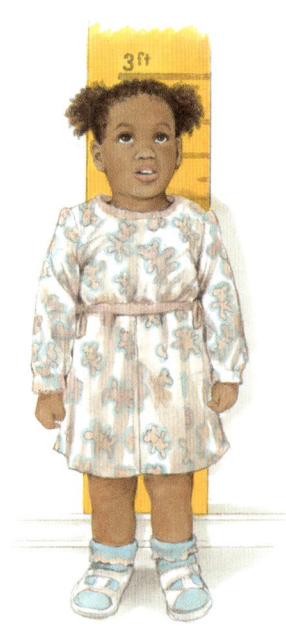

Place photo here.

Now that I'm older . . .

Place photo here.

My Family Tree

_____
Great-grandmother

_____
Great-grandmother

_____
Great-grandfather

_____
Great-grandfather

_____
Grandmother

_____
Grandfather

_____
Mom

_____
Me

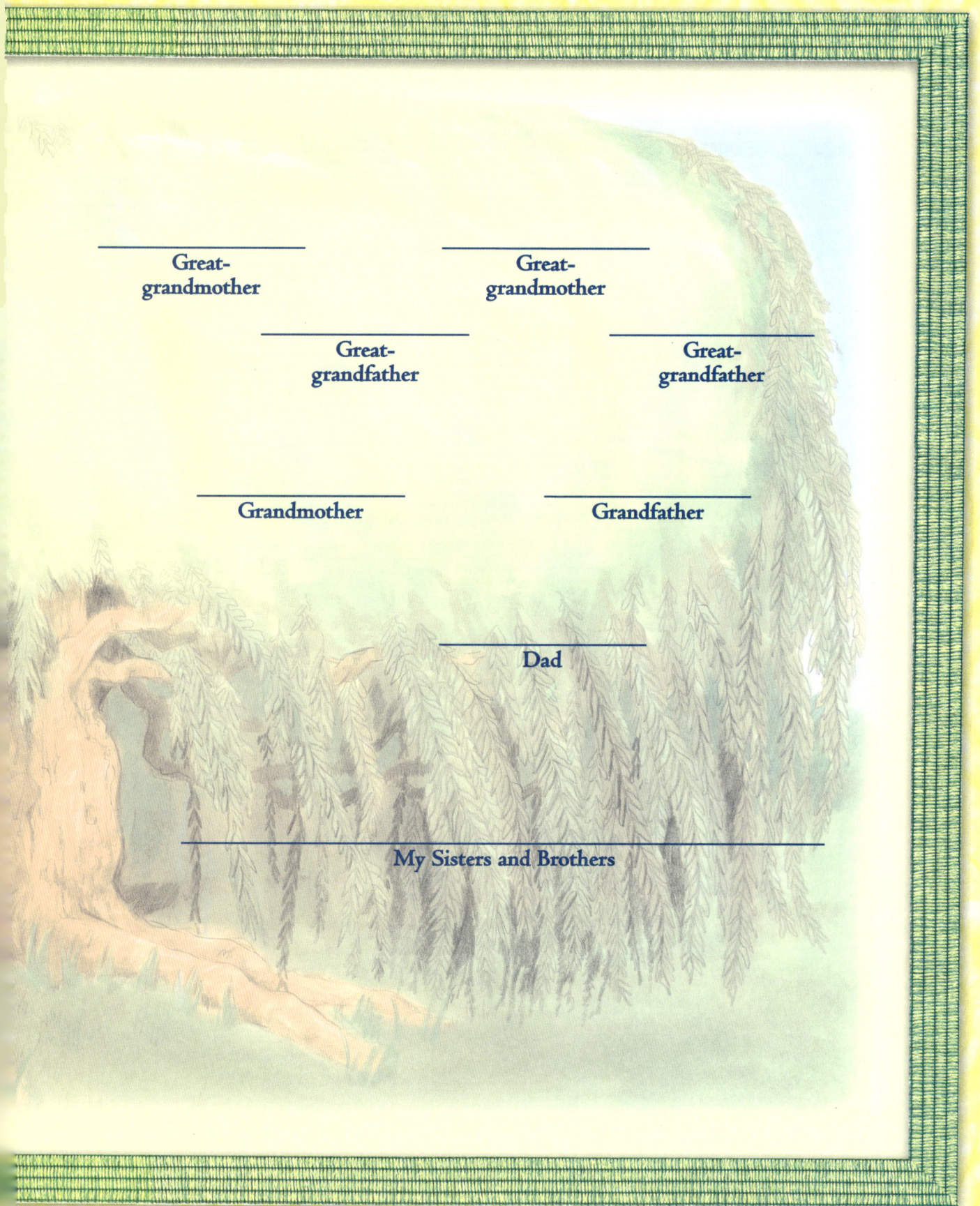

Great-
grandmother

Great-
grandmother

Great-
grandfather

Great-
grandfather

Grandmother

Grandfather

Dad

My Sisters and Brothers

Family Reunion

When my family gets together, we like to_____
_____
_____ .

I always have a good time when we're together because_____
_____
_____ .

Here are some other important members of my family:

Aunts _____
_____
_____

Uncles _____
_____
_____

Cousins _____
_____
_____

Godparents _____
_____
_____

Some close friends feel like family, even though they may not be related to me.
_____
_____
_____
_____

"My heritage is as beautiful and colorful as a hand-stitched quilt."
— courtesy *Gingersnaps* by Anita Alexander and Susan Payne

Family Photos

Back then . . .

Place photo here.

Place photo here.

And now . . .

Place photo here.

Place photo here.

My Home

Sunny or dark,
Big or small,
Yellow or red,
Short or tall.

A room.
A house.
An apartment.
A space.
No matter the size, if *home* is the place.

I live at_____

(address)

with_____

(with whom I live)

_____

_____

_____

_____

_____.

My favorite thing about my home is_____

_____

_____

_____

_____.

My favorite hiding place at home is_____

_____

because_____

_____.

I have my own room / I share my room with_____.

(circle one)

My room is_____

_____

_____.

My favorite thing about my room is_____

_____.

If I could paint my room any color, I'd paint it_____.

I am messy/neat. (circle one)

Soul Food

I love to eat_____
_____
_____
_____.

Ugh! I don't like eating_____
_____
_____.

Soul food is the history of my family as told through recipes. My ancestors brought foods from Africa, like yams and black-eyed peas. Once in America, they created new recipes from food native to America at that time, like collard greens, sweet potatoes, and corn. Today we use these ingredients to make "soul food," foods like sweet potato pie, grits, Hoppin' Johns, and corn bread. Soul food is a special part of my family and my culture.

My favorite "soul foods" are_____
_____
_____
_____ .

If I could have anything I wanted for dinner, I'd have_____
_____
_____
_____ .

And for dessert I'd have_____
_____
_____
_____ .

And I'd *have* to drink_____ .

_____does the cooking in my house.

I know how to make_____ .
(your favorite food to cook)

Include a recipe of your favorite food to cook or eat.

My Friends

My best friend is_____.

I like my best friend because_____
_____
_____.

We do fun things together like_____
_____
_____
_____.

Sometimes we disagree about_____
_____
_____
_____.

My other friends' names are:

_____   _____
_____   _____
_____   _____
_____

Me and My Best Buddies

Place photo here.

Place photo here.

Place photo here.

Place photo here.

My School

The name of my school is_____.

I am in _____ grade.

I have_____teacher(s). Their names are_____
_____
_____
_____
_____
_____
_____.

My favorite teacher's name is_____.

The subjects I have are:

_____   _____
_____   _____
_____   _____
_____   _____

*"School is the right place for me to show off
how clever, curious, and bright I am."*
— courtesy *Gingersnaps* by Anita Alexander and Susan Payne

My favorite subject is_____ because _____.

I don't like_____class.

After school, I like to

_____
_____
_____
_____
_____.

My favorite part of the school day is_____.

My least favorite part of the school day is_____.

Place your favorite pictures from school here.
Include your class picture or a picture
of someone special at school.

$1 + 4 = 5$

My Hobbies

In my free time I like to _____
_____
_____
_____

because _____
_____ .

My other hobbies are _____
_____
_____
_____ .

Games and Sports

My favorite game to play is _____ .

My least favorite game to play is _____ .

I like to play with _____ .

(favorite play pal)

Musical Me

An instrument I know how to play is_____.

I would like to learn how to play_____.

Books, Books, Books

Some of my favorite books are:

_____

_____

_____

_____

"When I open a book, I open the door to grand adventures."
— courtesy *Gingersnaps* by Anita Alexander and Susan Payne

In these books, my favorite characters are_____
_____
_____
_____
_____

They are my favorites because_____
_____
_____.

My favorite place to read is_____.

The best time of day to read is_____
_____

because_____
_____
_____.

More About Me

Feelings

My happiest times are when I'm_____.

Grrr!! I get annoyed when _____.

I get sad when_____
_____
_____.

*"When I'm feeling down, I can try to fill my mind
with good, happy, funny thoughts."*
— courtesy *Gingersnaps* by Anita Alexander and Susan Payne

The things I like most about myself:
_____
_____
_____
_____
_____
_____

I would never change_____
_____
_____about me.

If I wanted to change something about me, I would change_____
_____.

I like it when people_____
_____
_____
_____.

I don't like it when people _____
_____
_____
_____
_____ .

The best day in my life was when _____
_____
_____
_____
_____ .

My absolute worst day ever was when _____
_____
_____
_____
_____ .

The best things in my life are _____
_____
_____
_____
_____ .

My most embarrassing moment was when _____
_____
_____
_____
_____ .

If I were a parent I would _____
_____
_____ .

If I were a parent I would *never* _____
_____
_____ .

The Me People See

The Skin I'm In

My color is perfect because_____
_____
_____
_____
_____
_____
_____
_____.

I love to wear my hair_____
_____
_____
_____
_____
_____
_____.

The clothes you'll *always* see me wearing are my_____
_____
_____
_____
_____.

But I'd *never* wear_____
_____
_____.

*"I love the skin I'm in. It covers me from head
to toe in beautiful shades of brown."*

— courtesy *Gingersnaps* by Anita Alexander and Susan Payne

Dreams and Goals

Some things I think a lot about are_____
_____
_____
_____
_____
_____
_____
_____
_____
_____
_____ .

The thing about me that I am most proud of is_____
_____
_____
_____
_____
_____
_____
_____
_____
_____
_____
_____ .

My dream is to become a_____
because_____
_____
_____
_____
_____
_____
_____
_____ .

Check It Out

My TWO most favorite things:

Movies _____   _____

Television Shows _____   _____

Actors and Actresses _____   _____

Sports Teams _____   _____

Athletes _____   _____

"When I win, everybody wins — Serena wins, my mom wins. . . .
It helps Serena . . . because when I win, I can tell her what I did to win."
— Tennis champion Venus Williams

Colors _____   _____

Animals _____   _____

Songs _____   _____

Singers _____   _____

Rappers _____   _____

Music Videos _____   _____

Video Games _____   _____

Websites _____   _____

Holidays

My favorite holiday is_____.
It is my favorite because_____
_____
_____
_____.

Juneteenth is celebrated every year on June 19th. It marks the day in 1865 when slaves in Texas were officially freed. Incredibly, this was two and a half years after Abraham Lincoln delivered the Emancipation Proclamation — the announcement that should have put an end to slavery in all of the United States.

My family celebrates these holidays:

_____
_____
_____
_____
_____
_____
_____
_____
_____
_____

Kwanzaa is the celebration of the harvest. Kwanzaa begins on December 26th and lasts seven days. Each day represents an important theme: unity, self-determination, working together, helping each other, purpose, creativity, and faith.

My family has special things we do during the holidays. Every year we_____

_____

_____

_____

_____

_____

_____

_____

_____.

A Glimpse of History

My heritage is rich. My ancestors were strong. They set the stage for the great things women did after them, and the even greater things I will do in my life. My heritage is rich, and the women who came before me were proud.

In 1773, Phillis Wheatley became one of the first black women to publish a book. Her writings influenced and inspired generations of women, including award-winning authors and poets like Toni Morrison and Alice Walker.

Though incredibly successful, Oprah Winfrey was not the first African American woman to become a high-powered businessperson. Almost one hundred years ago, Madame C. J. Walker became the first female African American millionaire in the United States by developing hair care products.

And just when you thought the sky was the limit . . . Dr. Mae Jemison proved we can go even farther than that, by becoming the first female African American astronaut. Dr. Jemison spent more than a week orbiting Earth in the space shuttle *Endeavour*.

My heritage is rich, and the women who came before me were proud.

African Americans I Admire

Famous Folks

I admire_____because he/she_____
_____
_____
_____
_____.

I admire_____because he/she_____
_____
_____
_____
_____.

People I Know

I admire_____because he/she_____
_____
_____
_____
_____.

I admire_____because he/she_____
_____
_____
_____
_____.

I admire_____because he/she_____
_____
_____
_____
_____.

"I celebrate Black History every day."

— courtesy *Gingersnaps* by Anita Alexander and Susan Payne

Celebrating me

Birthdays

My best birthday was when I turned_____years old.

Friends who celebrated with me:

_____
_____
_____
_____
_____
_____

It was so much fun! We_____
_____
_____
_____
_____
_____.

My best birthday present was_____
_____
_____.

At my dream birthday party we would have_____
_____
_____.

We would eat_____
_____.

I would invite_____
_____
_____.

My Favorite Vacation

We went to_____.

We stayed at_____.

Family members and friends who came:
_____
_____

This was the best vacation because
_____
_____.

If I could travel anywhere in the world I would go to_____
_____

because_____
_____
_____
_____
_____.

Seasons

The season I like most of all is_____.

I love this time of year because_____.

Winter

When winter comes, I know it's time for_____
_____.

I love winter because_____
_____.

I don't like winter because_____
_____.

Spring

Springtime is great! Spring is my favorite time to_____

_____.

I like spring because_____

_____.

The thing I don't like about spring is_____

_____.

Summer

Summer is so much fun. When summer comes I get ready for_____
_____.

The thing I like to do most in the summer is_____
_____.

But I don't like_____
about summertime.

Fall

Fall is fun. The best thing about fall is_____

_____.

I wish fall lasted longer so I could_____

_____.

I'm glad when fall ends because it means_____

_____.

Addresses of My Friends and Family

Name_____
Address_____
City_____
State_____Zip Code_____
Phone_____
E-mail_____

Name_____
Address_____
City_____
State_____Zip Code_____
Phone_____
E-mail_____

Name_____
Address_____
City_____
State_____Zip Code_____
Phone_____
E-mail_____

Name_____
Address_____
City_____
State_____Zip Code_____
Phone_____
E-mail_____

Name_____
Address_____
City_____
State_____Zip Code_____
Phone_____
E-mail_____

Name_____
Address_____
City_____
State_____Zip Code_____
Phone_____
E-mail_____

Name_____
Address_____
City_____
State_____Zip Code_____
Phone_____
E-mail_____

Name_____
Address_____
City_____
State_____Zip Code_____
Phone_____
E-mail_____

Name_____
Address_____
City_____
State_____Zip Code_____
Phone_____
E-mail_____

Name_____
Address_____
City_____
State_____Zip Code_____
Phone_____
E-mail_____

Name_____
Address_____
City_____
State_____Zip Code_____
Phone_____
E-mail_____

Name_____
Address_____
City_____
State_____Zip Code_____
Phone_____
E-mail_____